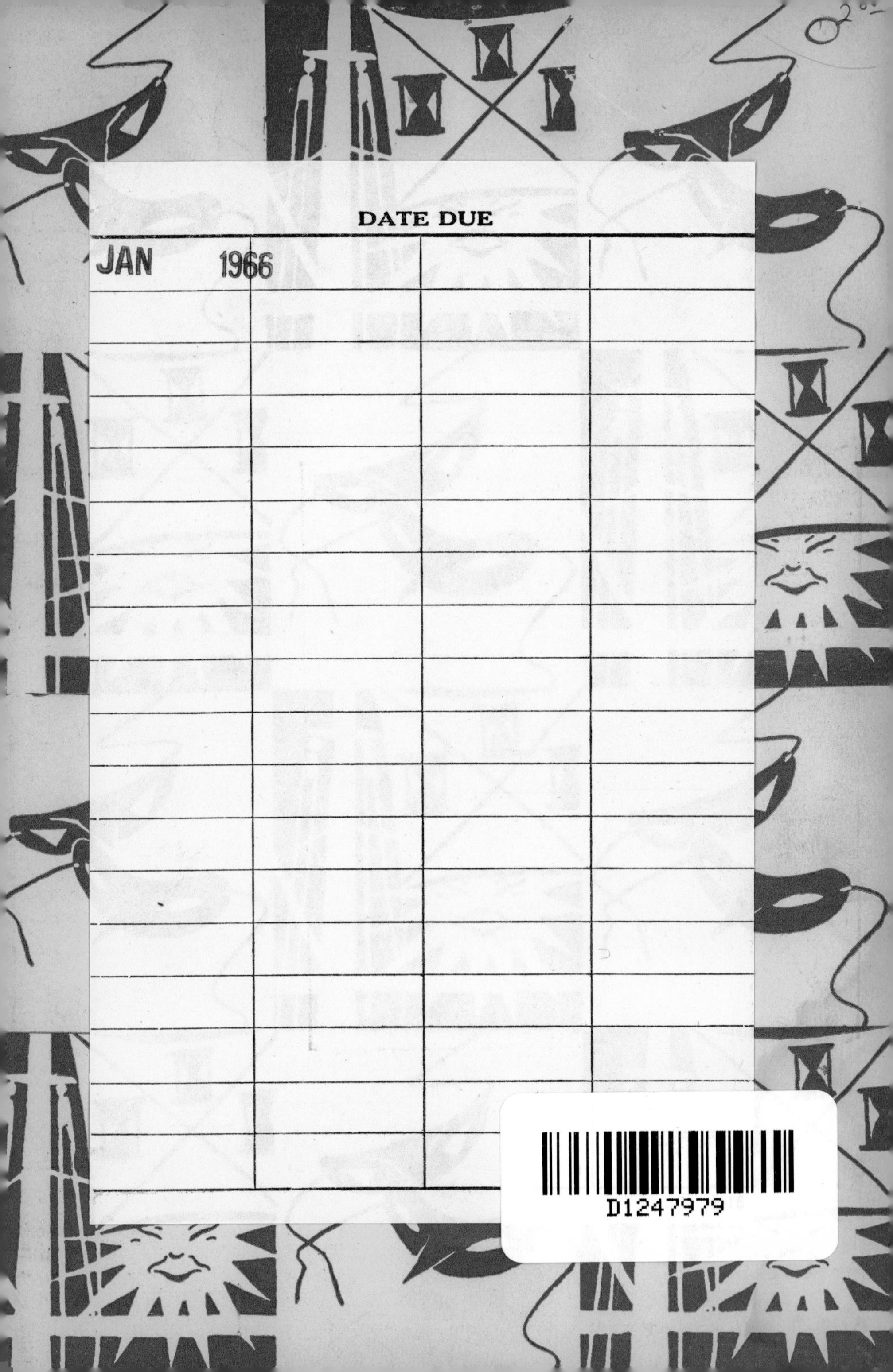
DATE DUE

JAN 1966

D1247979

SEACOAST OF BOHEMIA

From the Library of
Hugh B. Downey

For Chris Morley
with regards –
John A. Maxwell
J. Maxwell
C. Morley's Theatre – Dec. 13 · 1928

SEACOAST OF BOHEMIA

By Christopher Morley

Published for
The Old Rialto Theatre
118 Hudson Street, Hoboken, New Jersey
by
Doubleday, Doran and Company, Inc.
Garden City – 1929

COPYRIGHT, 1929
BY DOUBLEDAY, DORAN & COMPANY, INC.
COPYRIGHT, 1928
BY THE NEW YORK TIMES CO.
COPYRIGHT, 1928
BY THE SATURDAY REVIEW CO., INC.
COPYRIGHT, 1928
BY THE PRESS PUBLISHING CO.
ALL RIGHTS RESERVED
PRINTED IN THE UNITED STATES AT
THE COUNTRY LIFE PRESS
GARDEN CITY, N. Y.

FIRST EDITION

792
M864s

PREFACE

THE stage is loved, and men and women suffer in her service, with a passion unequalled in any other art. The reason for that is obvious: the stage is at once the most living and the most perishable of all forms of pretence. A theatre is born anew, and dies again, with every performance. No book of words, however lovingly compiled, can reproduce or perpetuate its essence. No amount of publicity nor high resolve nor expense of capital can galvanize it into life unless there is in the performance and in the house itself that mysterious magnetic vitality for which there is no substitute. The soul of the theatre exists only during those few hours, the brief fruit of long planning, while the lights are

KANSAS CITY (MO.) PUBLIC LIBRARY
6508708

on and an audience is there. The rest is mere anatomy. A French producer once wrote to an American dramatist whose play he had produced in Paris, trying with all the charm of his race to soften the bad news he had to transmit. "It was a fine play," he wrote, "and all the critics praised it, but the public postponed coming."

That was an immortal delicacy of phrase. If the public Postpones Coming, you have to fold up, and the quicker the better, whether you are Shakespeare, Sheridan, or Shaw. (Sh is evidently a lucky beginning for a dramatist's name.)

In spite of the quite unexpected nature of our foray into Hudson County, the generous public did not Postpone Coming. We have found in the Old Rialto and its surroundings the possibilities of a kind of adventure that no one else is attempting. The innermost flavor of so personal a place as a theatre cannot be conveyed in mere print. But in the hope of suggesting to a few kind patrons and friends what the old house means to us, and also with the not unworthily selfish desire of preserving a few souvenirs of our own, we have compiled this little book.

"Man comes into life to seek and find his sufficient beauty" was once suggested as a quotation (we don't know where it comes from) appropriate to place over the proscenium of a theatre. That may seem to you too lofty a mood to apply to a venture both humble and hilarious. But even in a pagan old theatre long forgotten by the Best People we have found moments of great pride and pleasure, and beauty sufficient to our condition.

The original predecessor of the Rialto, and (so far as we know) the first theatre on this site, was Weber's Germania Garden, erected about 1863. It was a two-story building, numbered 68–74 Hudson Street (the street-numbers have since been altered) and had a beer-garden adjoining. The ground floor was used for vaudeville performances, the hall upstairs for meetings and dancing. Among the earliest performers were a pair remembered now only as the Mullers; part of the attraction of this team was that the lady had very short skirts and rather massive legs in white stockings. Their specialty was a song beginning

Every night about half past eight
I hear someone knocking at my garden gate.

Some time in the early '80's, no one knows just when, the Germania Garden became Wareing's Theatre, from which time numerous delightful old playbills have been preserved. Wareing was evidently ambitious, for about 1887 he built another theatre in the next block on Hudson Street, which still exists under the name of the Lyric. Siegfried Cronheim presently took over the senior house, restoring its original name of the Germania. There is some confusion in the records and it cannot positively be stated whether Hoboken's greatest dramatic evenings took place in Wareing's new house or in the older one. There are partisans of both theories. What is certain is that in April, 1887, Mrs. Langtry appeared on Hudson Street for a week in three plays: *The Lady of Lyons*, *A Wife's Peril*, and *Pygmalion and Galatea*. Those were the great days of the Hoboken stage. Among other attractions of '87 and '88 were Bronson Howard's *The Banker's Daughter*, Hoyt's *A Parlor Match*, Kate Claxton and Charles Stevenson in *The Two Orphans*, Edwin Thorne in *The Black Flag*. Harrigan and Hart played here, and Weber and Fields in their salad days, billed far down the variety list as knockabout comedians in *The Crazy Dutchman*. Another star was Mme Janauschek, who was programmed as having "power and emotional force greater than Ristori, a nervous and fiery intensity equal to Rachel, and a skill for elaboration and finish only equalled by Sarah Bernhardt."

Just which of these glories took place in what is now the Rialto, and which in the neighboring Lyric, remains doubtful. When Wareing resigned the older house to Cronheim, that worthy met the competition with Teutonic vigor. Mr. Henry Hart, after careful study of the scrapbooks in the Hoboken Library, reports that even prize fights were staged among the beer tables of the Germania during the Cronheim régime. A reminiscent citizen signing himself OLD TIMER, recalling the Cronheim era in the Jersey *Observer* of December 20, 1921, specially mentions "a large Juno-like woman" who sang only in German, and who was sometimes accompanied by a Robert Ganzberg, who had a show of his own around on Washington Street between First and Second streets, and who, "Old Timer" declared, was the father of thirty children.

"But the peer of all who sang," writes this humble antiquarian, "was a young colored girl of possibly twenty years, slim and rather good looking, and with a truly beautiful voice. She would stand on the stage serene and self-possessed and sing, apparently without any effort. Her voice was rich, clear and full-throated. Its liquid melody affected even the most callow among her audience. Years later she was known as the Black Patti, but she had then become temperamental and would break her engagements."

The old Wareing programs advertised "A café in a tunnel under the theatre," and stated that "Ladies visiting the theatre without escort will be treated with the greatest courtesy." Another note was "It is earnestly requested that the patrons of this theatre will refrain from eating peanuts, it mars the performance and annoys the audience." The decoration on the first page of the program was a head of Shakespeare with the traditional Comic and Tragic masks beneath it—which still exist on the façade of the present Rialto. The Wareing program adds that "Attachés are not allowed to applaud the performance."

No one knows when Cronheim abandoned the house. Some time during the '90's the name was changed to the Empire. The house was rebuilt in 1902, and continued under the name of the Empire until a few years ago, playing burlesque, vaudeville, and stock.

We are under grateful obligation to the *Saturday Review of Literature* for allowing us to reprint three articles which appeared in that magazine under the dates of September 8, October 13, and November 24, 1928; and to Mrs. Nina Hatfield, the librarian of the Hoboken Public Library, who very kindly placed her files at our disposal. It should be added that the *Prologue for the Rialto Theatre* first appeared in print in the NEW YORK TIMES of November 25, 1928. Very special thanks are due to Mr. R. C. Rimington, Mr. John Alan Maxwell and Miss Jeanette Warmuth, who undertook the designing and illustrating of this little book.

CONTENTS

A PROLOGUE

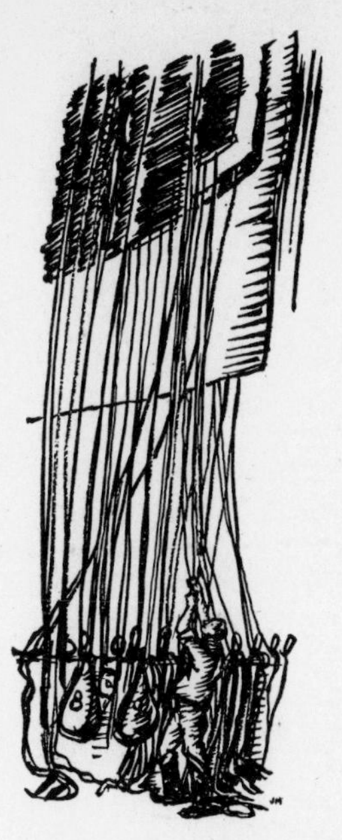

A PROLOGUE

FOR THE RIALTO THEATRE, HOBOKEN

LIGHTS, Henny!*
And then Henny gives us lights
To illustrate our new Hoboken Nights.
Now for a moment, while there hangs between us
Our favorite Psyche at the Court of Venus,**
A word before the ancient canvas rises.

*Henry Kuntze, the electrician.
**The painting on the curtain.

What is it that our curtain symbolizes?
Suggestions have been made, conjectures vain,
Interpretations sacred and profane:
The Muse of Movies, suppliant for her sins?
The Spirit seeking Where the Blue Begins?
Perhaps the Nymph of Cocktails we have here
Abashed before the Purity of Beer.
At least the blazon painted down below***
Is understandable and apropos—
Three hour-glasses: three hours of relaxation . . .
The other emblem**** needs no explanation.
And see the little peephole, noting how
The cloth is stained by many a moistened brow
Where the Manager, the Drama's anxious spouse,
Peered and perspired and counted up the house.

The curtain brightens, and this well-loved place
Lifts by some magic into finer grace:
By rich tradition of the trouper's trade,
By memories of all who here have played,
By love and laughter, in her frolic age
She brews us the pure Lethe of the stage.

***Insignia of the Three Hours for Lunch Club.
****A seidel of beer, symbolizing Hoboken.

There is no moonlight sweeter than her spots,
Her footlights burn with something more than
watts—
For all who face that mystic line of fire
Rise for the moment past all mean desire;
Beyond that radiant nimbus in the air
There might be all the world, or no one there
The greenest extra in the smallest bit
Knows he's immortally alone with it;
The most habitual ego, greedy elf,
Responds to something greater than himself—
This is the Highest Common Factor
And special honor of the actor.

Our Hudson Street, investigation yields,
Was once the site of the Elysian Fields
And still preserves, adventurers have found,
The humors of that famous picnic ground.
Here, free from Mazda Lane's monoxide scent,
Without New York's huge profit—and huge
rent—
Here, on this last unspoiled Bohemian coast,
We staked our claim, ejaculating Pros't!
But humble as we are, we have our pride:

One night we hung the S. R. O. outside.
The merriest antics shown upon this scene
Could not be happier than we have been.
Consider, if our scheme surprises you,
That Shakespeare played Across the River too.

Time to ring up! I add, to close these rhymes,
That we were christened, by THE NEW YORK
TIMES,
"A merger of Thalia and Gambrinus."
What rôle more pleasing could the gods assign us?
Whether you come for drama or for beer,
Whether you come from far away or near,
Remember, in apportioning your bounty,
The only legit house in Hudson County—
Remember, in your evenings unbespoken,
The Old Rialto Theatre, Hoboken!

ADVENTURE IN HOBOKEN

OCCASIONALLY someone inquires What has become of the Three Hours for Lunch Club? It is true that its activities have more privacy nowadays than when (how long ago it seems) they served as filler for a daily newspaper column. But no one need suppose that the Club—

once editorially described by no less a journal than the Baltimore *Sun* as "the world's most civilized institution"—has suffered any demise. Its members, some of them growing perhaps a little stouter or a little grayer, meet less often in plenipotentiary session; but it still preserves all the quixotry of its youth. One function of the Club, you may remember, was every now and then to devote its energies to some Great Cause. It has not been forgotten that once upon a time the club bought and saved from destruction a full-rigged ship. The ambition to start a chop-house on Ann Street was never fulfilled, because that old courtyard and smithy (the most relish-able bit of early New York that our generation will remember) was torn down and built over. But now the club has a new Cause, and though it has kept pretty quiet about it there's no reason why the news shouldn't leak out. The Club has leased a theatre and gone in for producing.

I almost hesitate to tell you where; for this theatre is in the last seacoast of Bohemia that is left in New York, unpolluted by sophistication. We don't want it spoiled by the prematurely knowing. For this is not a "little" theatre, nor an "arty" theatre nor an "amateur" theatre nor a theatre in a cellar or a stable or a wharf or an attic. It is one of the last of the oldtime playhouses of this region, a house redolent with rich showman atmosphere, strong with the color and gaudy make-believe of the stage of fifty years ago. The echoes of many generations of troupers are in it, and the aromatic savour of thousands of nights of melodrama and burlesque. The old Bowery flavour that, they tell me, Mae West has sought to recapture in *Diamond Lil* is obvious in this playhouse's very fabric. The woes and hokums of sixty years of playing have been trodden into the scuffed old stage and breathe in the scribbled ribaldries on the walls of the old prop room. There is even a ghost, I dare say, for there's a legend of a Leading Lady who fell through the ancient trap. I say sixty years at random, for so far no one in Hoboken has been able——

I've given it away; but I was going to anyhow.

★

Long ago, for reasons entirely their own, certain members of the Club formed a habit of occasionally going over to Hoboken for lunch. The old joke about Hoboken being foreign territory had some truth in it, you stepped off at the other end of the ferry and found yourself in a delightfully different world. There were ships, and quiet streets sunning themselves in a noonday doze, and comfortable German hotels where men sat lingeringly at their meals. One walked up the hill to Stevens Institute and looked out over the great panorama of New York—an honoured member of the Club, Mr. Muirhead Bone, did a magnificent drawing of that prospect. In the early days of the Club's rambles in Hoboken the *Leviathan* still lay there, dingy and derelict, a memento of bad times. There was a Greek confectioner named Pappanicholas, whom we suspected of being the actual Santa Claus. There was, and still is, an authentic German bookshop —*Buchhandlung*. On warm days then, as now, the firemen on Hudson Street would turn on the hydrant with a special spray attachment, and not only children but grown-ups too bathed happily in the misty shower. And near that same hydrant was a frolicsome old theatre with which, though

HOBOKEN, N. J., MONDAY, April 18th, and during the week.

JULIUS SCHLATTER'S
RESTAURANT,
No. 42 HUDSON STREET.
WARM MEALS from 7 A. M. to 9 P. M.

"THE RESORT"
Corner Newark & Hudson Sts.
"CON" J. DONOVAN, PROPRIETOR.

M. P. WHELAN,
SCENIC ARTIST
with J. S. MAGUIRE,
Sign & Banner Painter,
34 WASHINGTON ST., HOBOKEN.

For a long time it has been a practice among Furniture Dealers to sell on the instalment plan. They have reaped a rich harvest; and why? because they have charged about double what the goods were really worth. Those good times for the Furniture Dealers are over.

Since H. CORDTS has started his
NEW STORES & AUCTION ROOMS,
Nos. 66 & 98 FIRST STREET,
BET. PARK & WILLOW AVES., HOBOKEN, N. J.
he has marked all his Furniture at very low prices, and offers the same, if desired, on weekly payments.
Also Carpets, Oil Cloths, Beddings, Baby Carriages, Oil Paintings, etc., at very low prices.
Second-hand Furniture taken in exchange. Furniture and other merchandise taken on Storage and money advanced on same.
Upholstering and Repairing done at shortest notice.
H. Cordts, Auctioneer.

F. CORDTS,
76 and 83 Washington Street.
HOBOKEN, N. J.
FURNITURE AND CARPETS ON TIME.
Storage Taken.

Week of April 18th, 1887

Monday, Tuesday, Wednesday & Thursday Nights,
THE
Wages of Sin Company.

Friday & Saturday Nights and Sat'day Matinee,
SPECIAL ENGAGEMENT OF
MRS. LANGTRY,
—IN HER REPERTOIRE OF—
A WIFE'S PERIL,
LADY OF LYONS,
PYGMALION & GALATEA.

LANGTRY'S SCALE OF PRICES:
Reserved Seats, $1.00 and $1.50. General Admission, Fifty Cents.

Sunday Night and Matinee, April 24th,
THE GALLEY SLAVE

NEXT WEEK.
The Eminent Actor, Mr. EDWIN THORNE,
—IN—
THE BLACK FLAG!

THEATRE CAFÉ,
DOWN STAIRS, UNDER THE THEATRE.
Fine Wines, Liquors & Segars.
RUPPERT'S EXTRA LAGERBEER.
A. CHRISTOPH, Proprietor.

GAS CONSUMERS,
—CAN SECURE—
33⅓ PER CENT REDUCTION
—IN—
GAS BILLS.
Greater Brilliancy of Light,
STEADIER FLAME
Security Against Fire.
No Blowing nor Smoking Burners!
No Broken Globes!
Insurance Risks Greatly Reduced!
MARVELLOUS SANITARY EFFECTS!
The Union National Gas Saving Co.,
21 E. 14th Street, New York.

These Machines are Used in this Theatre.
I recommend them to all Gas Consumers, as they have saved me at least 33 per cent.
ROB'T WARING.

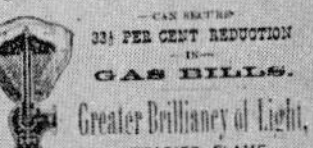

Wilhelm Karle's
Restaurant and Hotel,
125 Washington Street.
Corner Third Street, HOBOKEN, N. J.
Rooms by the Day or Week. Prices Reasonable.
Special rates to Professionals, with or without Board.

THE HOBOKEN COAL COMPANY.

Dealers in SCRANTON, HAZLETON, OLD COMPANY'S LEHIGH, SUSQUEHANNA WHITE AND RED ASH, ALLIANCE RED ASH AND OTHER COALS.
Families supplied with carefully selected Coal, at the lowest rates. Manufacturers' orders promptly filled.
BITUMINOUS COAL FOR BLACKSMITHING. INCE HALL AND PETERSBURGH CANNEL.

YARDS:—Grove, cor. 19th St., Jersey City, and 5th St., between Grove & Henderson, Jersey City.
OFFICES:—At the Yards; 111 Broadway, Room 40, New York; 101 Montgomery Street, Jersey City; Cor. Bay St. & Newark Ave., Jersey City; Pier 10, Hoboken Coal Dock.
General Office,
Bank Bldg., cor. Newark & Hudson Sts.
P. O. Box 247. Telephone at all Offices.

we suspected it not, the Club's destiny was connected.

★

The credit—if there should be any credit—belongs primarily to Mr. Cleon Throckmorton, the eminent stage designer, who happened in at the Rialto Theatre in Hoboken because a former employee of his was playing a "bit" there; and his unrivalled eye for theatre effects fell in love with the glamorous old house. He laid his ideas before some of his colleagues in the Club; heads were put together; through a long season of mint-julep meetings (the Club's official beverage in warm weather) the pros and cons of the problem were discussed. In short, a lease was signed; behold, in the warm days of August, Mr. Throckmorton himself engaged with a paintbrush; and the old auditorium emerging from grime and peanut-shells into a lively vision of gold and white and scarlet not unreminiscent (so the wiseacres say) of the famous Deutsches Theater in Berlin. Not since the era of the old Wallack's have I seen (in New York) a playhouse that speaks so irresistibly to the lover of the stage's oldest tricks.

★

We have always been quite candid, unprofitably candid, in such comments on the Club's affairs as have been made public. There was one

division of the managing committee that argued vigorously against New York being informed at all of this transfluminal venture. It was Hoboken's affair entirely, they said; it was intended for the long-standing clientele of the old Rialto, and not for explorers. They said that if people knew how agreeable it is to slip aboard the ferry at 23rd Street (enjoying the lights and fresh air of the river, instead of the traffic and monoxide fumes of Times Square), and then find themselves within a few paces of the theatre, that the house would be thronged with smart New Yorkers looking for a new sensation. There were many other reasons alleged why it would be better not to let anyone into the secret; with most of which I heartily agree. But after all the Club has never been selfish; and the kind of people who read the *Saturday Review* can be trusted to be discreet. It would be a pity if people reproached us afterward for not having told them. One of the oddest things about humanity is its habit of trapesing along the same steady groove. Far too seldom do we hear anyone get up and say, apropos of nothing, Let's go to New Utrecht and see what happens there; or Long Island City; or Jamaica (L. I.); or—well, Hoboken. A man who one day had an impulse to go and study Newark (a very amazing town, incidentally) is more genuinely a traveller than one who gets aboard a swell steamer and goes to the neighborhood of the Place Vendôme, just because the shipping companies kept telling him to do so. Or, to take another example, Eighth Avenue, all this summer, in the throes of excavation, has been a spectacle thrilling beyond words, incredible, magnificent. To trudge along there, once a week or so, and observe that stupendous ugly panorama of savage toil and calculated confusion is an education in Futurity. Not the niftiest window-décor of Fifth Avenue nor the wildest modernism of designers has given me so clear a punctuation of what the world is going to be like.

It would be an impertinence to remark here what eventual hopes or intentions had these well-wishing adventurers in setting forth. But it would equally have been a misdemeanor not to apprise a righteous few that the sacred traditions of melodrama and farce can still be found in a theatre that looks like a theatre—the kind of theatre that in London would be named (after a pub) the Elephant and Castle. For the moment it *is* our Castle: it may yet prove to be our Elephant.

But if you come to look at our last seacoast of

Bohemia you must bring your own eyes with you, and not see it through anyone else's, nor with any

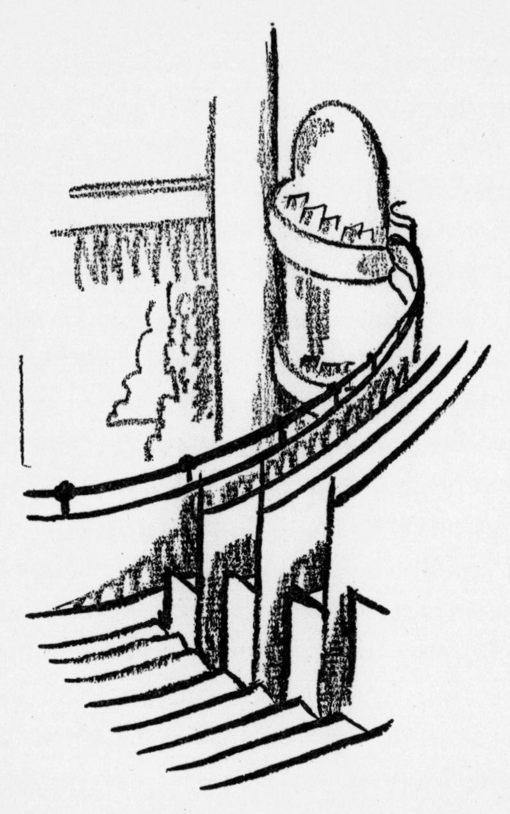

preconceived notions of what is or isn't picturesque. Suppose you go by the Holland Tunnel or the Hudson Tubes, even those alone are miracles enough for one evening, aren't they? How often do you smell that whiff of the Hudson ferries which ought to be the birthright of every New Yorker? Crossing rivers was always thought to be symbolic; there was the Rubicon, the Jordan, the Delaware, the Styx. Even Shakespeare played Across the River, in Southwark—which explains a great deal in his work.

But that's no parallel: for if you come (the no-publicity faction asked me to say) don't bring with you any dramatic critics or highbrows or people who go to the theatre just to have their withers wrung with Dostoievsky and "Dusty Answer." Allow half an hour from Times Square. Matinées Wednesdays and Saturdays!

THE CURTAIN

AT THIS very moment, as I sit down to write (twenty minutes past eight P. M.), someone is probably looking through the peep-hole. Someone, while the stage is being set for the first act and the prop-list is checked over, is undoubtedly stealing a glimpse through that little eyelet in the curtain to see what the house looks like. If you are attentive to details and happen to sit where you can remark that small orifice, you will see that the old painted canvas is faintly stained just round it. That is due, I suppose, to the moisture on the anxious brows of generations of managers as they peered hopefully or fearfully through and mentally estimated the take.

I wish I could tell you more about that curtain. Theatre curtains might well be thematic for an essay on the arts in general; they would excellently symbolize the necessity, true in every department, of having some dividing line of illusion which conceals from the world what is not intended to be seen; or if seen, not acknowledged. That is the kind of floral farrago that everyone enjoys writing, and is easiest to write. But I am thinking chiefly of one particular curtain, very dear to me—that in the old Rialto Theatre in Hoboken.

I wish again that I could tell you more about it. The difficulty is that I am short-sighted, and raerly get a chance to have a good look at it. For of course it is only down during performances, at which times it is not seemly for a myopic manager to go boldly down the middle aisle and study it. It has been described as a "bastard Alma Tadema," which is fairly (though not completely) accurate. At any rate it is precisely in the mode of thirty or forty years ago when the supreme requisite of a theatre curtain was that it should tell a story. The question is, what story does it tell? There is a lady sitting on a throne above a flight of marble steps. At the bottom of these steps, considerably unclad, another lady is spread out in an attitude of shame or supplication. There are still other damsels standing about; and I think (as well as I have been able to discern, in moments of agitation) a suggestion of classic cypress trees. The suppliant and unclad lady has a multitude of auburn hair which is dishevelled beneath her prone and comely person. If it were a contemporary painting I might be tempted to believe that she represents the Muse of Hollywood, now terrified by movietone developments, beseeching the Muse of Old Comedy to grant pardon for her sins.

There is a legend in Hoboken that this famous old curtain illustrates an episode in Tennyson's *Princess. The Princess* is a poem which, considered as narrative, I have never been patient enough to grasp; though like anyone in his senses

I relish its magnificent interpolations of epigram and lyric. It was so promptly accepted, I believe, as effective propaganda for the New Womanhood that ladies hardly paused long enough to observe how jocundly Tennyson chaffed them here and there in the poem. What better description has ever been given of a certain kind of excitable feminine handwriting—

> *In such a hand as when a field of corn*
> *Bows all its ears before the roaring East.*

It is exquisitely humorous to consider this Tennysonian and feminist curtain used during the years of the old Rialto's decadence to intermission the rumpish charms of Hoboken burlesque shows.

But if this jolly old canvas illustrates *The Princess*, as alleged, still I am too short-sighted to identify which special episode of the poem is conveyed. Is it the passage where someone is told

> *Marsh-divers shall croak thee, sister,*

or is it the scene where behind the Princess stand

> *Eight daughters of the plough, stronger than men,*
> *Huge women blowzed with health.*

That indeed would be accurate enough for the days of the burlesque wheel. Or does it represent

Half naked as if caught at once from bed
And tumbled on the purple footcloth, lay
The lily-shining child; and on the left,
Her round white shoulders shaken with her sobs,
Melissa knelt—

But whatever phase of *The Princess* that canvas may portray, I leave to more accomplished Tennysonians to divine—hoping only that the manager, peering through his peephole, may not

have occasion to murmur the most famous of *The Princess's* lyrics—

Tiers, idle tiers, I know not what they mean.

★

Hoboken, like many another faubourg adjacent to proud cities, has been much misunderstood. "The very convenient, but unlovely city of Hoboken," says my old friend the 1898 Rand McNally Guide to New York which is one of my favourite antiquarian works. But I wish I could take Messrs. Rand and McNally for a stroll along Hudson Street, Hoboken, some sunny autumn afternoon; past those comfortable old Teuton hotels, across the little park which was once the famous Elysian Fields, up to the airy parnassus of Castle Stevens. There, in the tower of that astonishing old mansion, is what I assert to be the most spectacular eyrie in Greater New York: the pensive citadel where Dr. H. N. Davis, the new president of Stevens Institute, works late at night on his plans for the future of that fine college and looks abroad over the most remarkable panorama in modern civilization. The view of New York from Brooklyn Heights is fairly well-known; how much less we hear of the wider synopsis from Castle Stevens. It is interesting to be told, since we concern ourselves just now with the drama, that the first open-air play ever performed in America was given on the campus of Stevens. The college is a scientific school, and (to quote our *Princess* again) mostly occupied with "the hard-grained Muses of the cube and square," but therefore all the more hospitable to the tenderer arts in its moments of relaxation. There, as you ramble about the grounds, you may ponder on the vision of American life which is spread out before those young men who are studying to be the engineers and builders of the future. Dr. Davis and I were imagining the superb amphitheatre which the Stevens cliff seems to have been intended to suggest—a theatre where the whole of Manhattan would serve as cyclorama—and we agreed that such a scheme would take us at least a hundred years to work out.

So, in that quiet air, there seems to be no desperate hurry. That tranquil and prosperous residential region behind Castle Stevens, only half an hour from down-town by tube or ferry, remains (by the happy accident of unprestige) unspoiled by the rent *schieber* and the social alpinist. In such a neighborhood, which we used to describe jocularly as Behind the Bayonne, did these enamored zealots set up their antics behind the painting of Lord Tennyson's legend. What gorgeous names—Hoboken, Weehawken, Communipaw! (It should not be forgotten that the word *Hoboken*, in some Indian lingo, meant a tobacco pipe.) And a lover of print may be excused for enthusiasm over the town called Gutenberg. In the cliff beneath Castle Stevens there was once a natural grotto known as the Sibyl's Cave. It was famous as cool cellarage for beer barrels. Neither the beer nor the sibyls have wholly deserted Hoboken.

★

But the Sibyl's Cave was also highly esteemed for a very fine spring of pure water. In the palmy days of the Elysian Fields, when all the Hoboken river front was a rustic picnic ground, a little classic temple was built round the spring; it be-

400 GLEASON'S PICTORIAL DRAWING-ROOM COMPAN

SYBIL'S CAVE, HOBOKEN, N. J.

Hoboken is beautifully situated in New Jersey, on the Hudson River, directly opposite the south end of New York City, and is, together with Staten Island, the quickest resort of the New Yorkers. You take the ferry at the foot of Barclay Street, Canal Street, or Christopher Street, and in five minutes you are in the country. Thousands visit this "paradise of Gotham," daily. The shore is wild and rocky; it is beautifully laid out into walks, promenades and parks, overshadowed by the richest foliage. It has one or two churches, several first-rate hotels, and contains a thousand or more regular inhabitants; it also possesses a very large ship yard. The whole is owned by W. L. Stevens, Esq., to whom belongs the immortality of not only making, but keeping the finest spot adjacent to any city in the world. Sybil's Cave, Hoboken, is one of the principal attractions of the place. No one visits Hoboken without seeing it. It is hewn out and excavated from a solid rock to the depth of thirty feet. In the middle is a spring of pure and sparkling water thousands of glasses of which are sold daily in the summer, for a penny per glass. The cave was designed by the owner, W. L. Stevens, Esq. In the engraving, Hudson River and Weehawken are seen in the distance. The small building adjoining is a place for refreshments.

SYBIL'S CAVE, AT HOBOKEN, N. J.

came a place of almost pious pilgrimage. Isn't it in one of Poe's stories (*Marie Roget*, perhaps: I haven't had a chance to look it up) that the arcadian charms of the Elysian Fields are described? Then the region became a favorite centre of athletic pastime. There were boating clubs, and fishing clubs, and clubs for the preparation and consumption of turtle soup. International cricket matches were played there (there is an old print of the United States Vanquishing

Canada in the leisurely game); and I have met young college men who are amazed to hear that the first Yale-Princeton football game took place in Hoboken. A hearty spirit of relaxation and sport was evidently part of the genius of the place. Places have their own instinctive character and temperament; not all the transformations of the past fifty years have been able to erase from Hoboken its strong sense of convivial fun.

Hoboken now stands on the sill of a new era, for that the next twenty years will show incredible changes no speculator in futures can doubt. It is interesting at such a time to glance back and see how different she was about the time our predecessor, the Germania Garden, began offering entertainment to the Elysian picnickers. In the New York Public Library, Cleon Throckmorton came across an odd little book of poems (presented to the Library, incidentally, by Paul Leicester Ford). It is called *Hoboken*, by Julia Julius, and was privately printed in 1866. The title-poem would be worth reprinting entire, but at least we can find space for two stanzas:—

VIEW OF HUDSON RIVER, FROM ELYSIAN FIELDS, HOBOKEN, NEW JERSEY

Fair Hoboken lies peaceful at our feet,
Her well kept gardens bright with flowers rare
Adorn each cottage, and in summer heat
Mingle their odors in the balmy air.
Those who from Gotham's turmoil would retreat
May wander far and not find aught so fair—
However, people very seldom prize
That which they daily have before their eyes.

We near the Sibyl's Cave, so let us pause
A draught of her elixir to obtain—
Come, quaff the sparkling liquid, it restores
Vigor and strength to body and to brain;

Its virtue to my mind deserves applause
Beyond Veuve Clicquot's world-renowned champagne
Because however freely you partake
You never have a headache when you wake.

★

There were sometimes evenings, during the first anxious days of experiment, when one looking through that hole in the old curtain might have thought a little enviously of times (described in yellowed clippings in the Hoboken Library) when as many as 40,000 people gathered in the Elysian Fields to make merry on Saturdays and Sundays. But whatever moments of anxiety there may have been, they never continued after one was actually inside that jocund old playhouse. There is in her, ingrained into her fabric by years of trouping, so fine a savor of old theatre essence, something of that humble but unmistakable glamour that comes only with years of laughter and trouble. Whatever a manager or a player thinks when he looks hopefully through the peephole he keeps it in his secret heart. And how important it is for every artist, of whatever métier, to have somewhere a secret chink through which, unsuspected, he can gaze out on the enormous world.

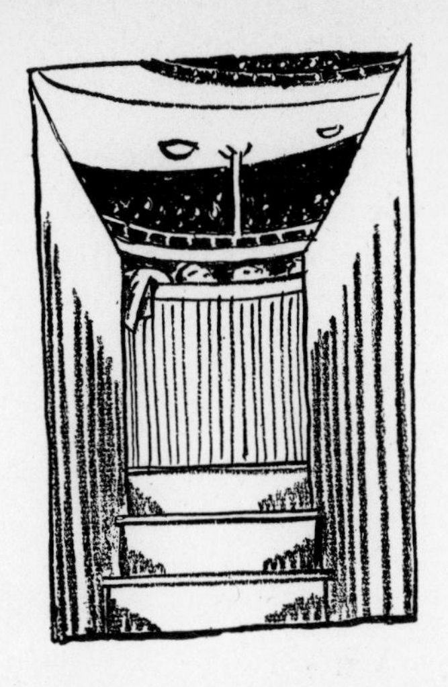

ELYSIAN FIELDS

THE life of actors and managers, in a stock company at least, gives them mercifully little time to think. For there are wise old precautions against being too sharply aware of the tissue of analogies that is our whole mental world. Only to oldest most compassionate friends does anyone confess his amazed and troubled apprehensions of loveliness. The actor when offstage is, I daresay, secretly aware of the exquisite symbolism of the theatre as a microscope of all civilized existence—that symbolism which so engaged the mind of the greatest Actor-Manager. But in his work the burning radiance of the footlights rises between the actor and the house, just as the dazzling urgency of To-day is always between man and Reality. He must not be aware of his audience—nor even of himself. The least seizure of introspection is fatal.

Such statements are absurd; but it is the beauty of all esthetic rules that they are absurd and impossible. By our freedom of manœuvre along the frontier of impossibility we exist as artists. The very greatest of Actor-Managers, we are told, was an atrocious performer. This was as it must be. A good Manager *should* be a bad actor. He should have too many things on his mind to make it possible for him to be a slick performer.

★

Surely it is that occasional dumb awareness of Perfect Analogy that is the actor's consolation. It is the more perfect because he rarely analyzes or admits it. Actors have (very rightly) organized an Equity Association to compel managers to fair play: and yet actors exist for the very purpose of having people be unfair to them. In short,

to accept other people's ideas and emotions and pretend to make them their own, which is surely the unfairest thing that can happen to a person. The relation of actor and director is perfect theology. With godlike assurance the director dictates movement and tone and business; and once the scene is "set" no conscientious performer would dream of transgressing the carefully arranged pattern; yet even within that pattern, as in the routine of life itself, there still must remain room for individual improvisation. Upon the actor's divinely childlike quality of faith and acceptance the whole convention depends. Perhaps only by entering (no matter how clumsily) into the actor's own task can the student of these affairs begin to realize the essential problem; that of preserving the perfect naïveté which is the artist's talisman. When he faces the footlights' mystic veil of fire he carries on his innocent shoulders the whole incredible weight of art. And this is the job that by the most fantastic misnomer in language they still call a "play."

★

There were certain kinds of evil magic, you remember, whose power could not cross running water. Perhaps that also is true of some sophistries and cynicisms of our present era. In a for-

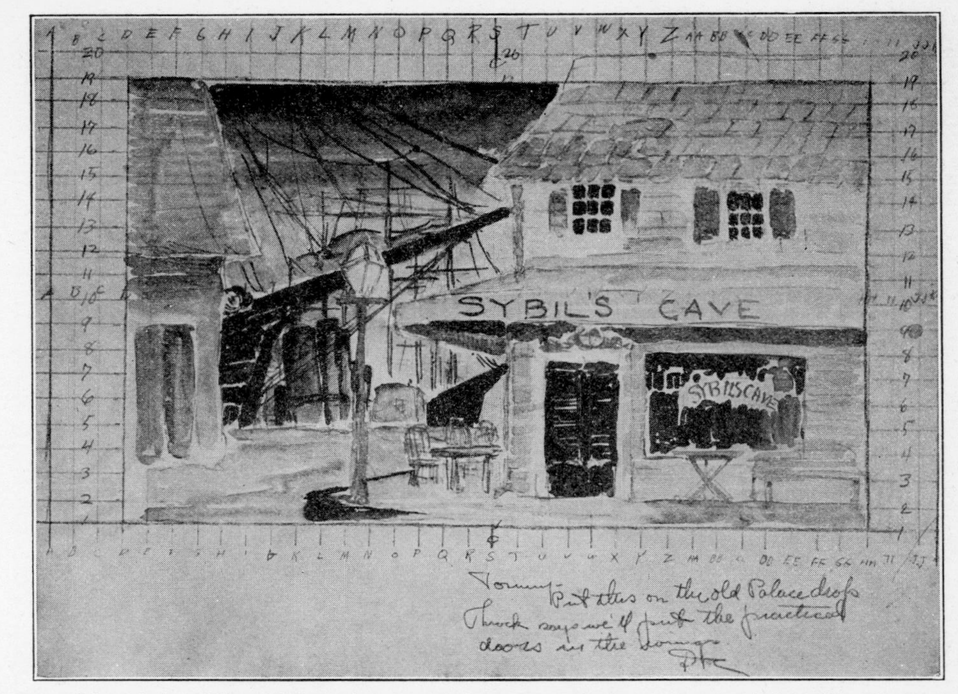

Sketch by Cleon Throckmorton for water-front drop in After Dark

gotten old playhouse across the Hudson even some who were trained to be skeptical found a reality to love and be thankful for. In that region of unimpaired simplicity, where even a dance-hall orchestra whoops with merriment as it crashes out its savage numbers, there is a sense of comedy worthy of the Tudors. It would need a Marlowe to tell the beauty of that queer old backstage cavern, its chequer of lights and shadows, the tense attitudes of those waiting for their cue. When is a human profile so appealing as just before it takes its cue? And imagine the excitement of a prentice performer who learned, in experiment with the art of make-up, that there is a grease-paint called *Juvenile Hero Flesh*. Alas that he will probably never be allowed to use it—

No wonder that the stock company, with all its innumerable anxieties and makeshifts, has been the nursery of so much that is finest in the theatre. It is the cradle of the incredible. By some miracle rehearsals actually take place, sets get built, what looked impossible suddenly falls into harmony, the show goes on. For a week or a fort-

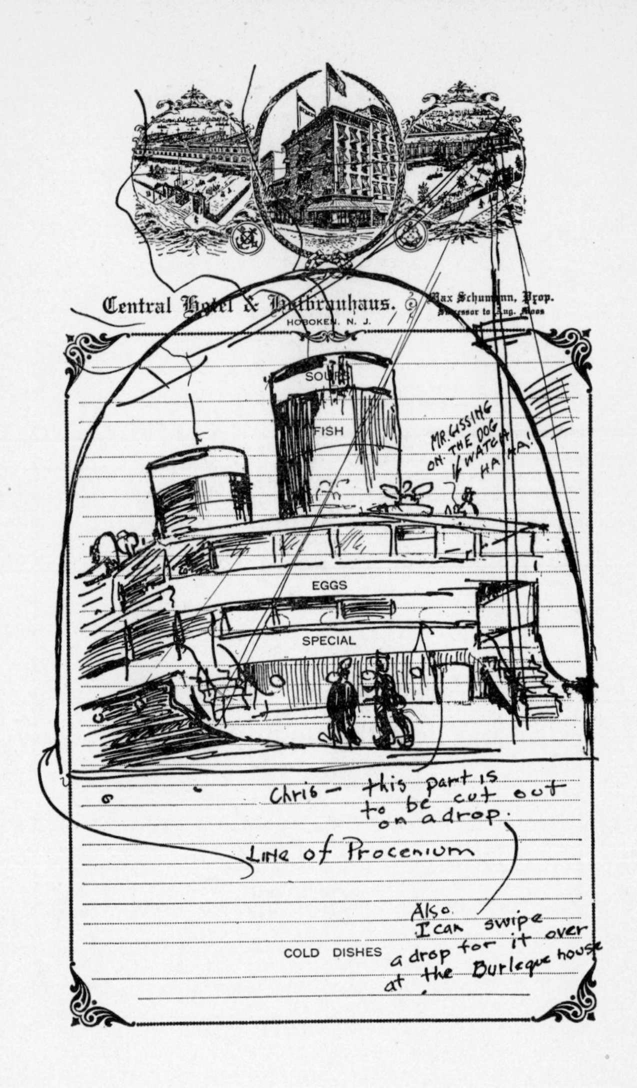
Central Hotel & Hofbrauhaus.
HOBOKEN, N. J.
SOUPS
FISH
EGGS
SPECIAL
COLD DISHES
MR. GISSING ON THE DOG WATCH HA HA!
Chris — this part is to be cut out on a drop.
Line of Procenium
Also. I can swipe a drop for it over at the Burleque house

Suggestion for
last Act of
Max Schumann, Prop.
Successor to Aug. Moos
BLUE
SOUPS
Profile furna
FISH
Light of fire.
EGGS
SPECIAL
Mr. Beagle

night, in the minds of that loyal and hilarious group, its fantastic pretences seem more real than the most urgent necessities of life. It is well to remember, a Stock Manager sometimes reminds himself, that the greatest Show of all only had six days' rehearsal.

★

I suppose that people born and reared in the theatre, or people in regions less Elizabethan than Hudson Street, Hoboken, would take the glamours of an antique playhouse more for granted and would be too tony to find beauty flourish in so mean a habit. Please be that some of us shall never take things for granted nor lose the jocund faculty of amazement. Sometimes, for respite from incredulity, the Walrus steps with the Carpenter into the back alley where by rapping at a barred and shuttered window a glass of beer is handed out into the night. You stand in the dark alley, and with the natural upward homage of the beer-drinker find your gaze upon a speckled glimmer of stars. That dark blank wall alongside you houses the whole blazing mimicry of the play; behind it, in your mind's ken, you see the company at their stations, bless their hearts, and the alert stage manager in his corner "on the book," and that pallid face peering through the red curtains far at the back of the house, the director watching with the eye of God. The clothes-masts that decorate the rear of the theatre, where Hudson Street hangs out its clothes on wash-day, rise up against the sky, and far away down the street is the yammer of the last of the German gutter-bands. A deep rumble sounds from within and Walrus and Carpenter look cheerfully at each other. "They seem to be liking it," says the Walrus. "Yes," replies the Carpenter. "A real belly-laugh. That's what I like to hear."

Yes, it is too reckless to tell others—except the very understanding and well discretioned—of beauties you may have seen. Perhaps we do not love things because they are beautiful; they are beautiful because we love them. But there are always many, the true Victorias, ready to be Not Amused. So we have learned already, not to tell people that our old Rialto is beautiful but simply to say that we love her. Touched, even in our own tenure of her, by tragedy, she holds not only her own long store of irretrievable memories but ours as well. But to have found, in the most herd-minded of all great cities, one playground that cannot conceivably be spoiled by psittacine and sophist, is perhaps a modest gift to an anxious civilization. It is pleasant to remember that it is in the region of the once famous Elysian Fields. Perhaps that is a worthy ambition: to revive the Elysian Fields. . . . Elysian Weber and Fields.

FROM A SCRAPBOOK

IT WOULD be too much to expect us to refrain, in so intimate a scrapbook as this, from reprinting a few extracts from some of the press clippings that have beguiled our early days. The episode of St. John Ervine and the pig's knuckle, for example, could not be allowed to remain in the mere privacy of the *World's* files. It would have been amusing to quote from an article in which a Manhattan journalist who syndicates for the provinces let on that he himself of course had been going to Hoboken for years; but alas he gave himself away by saying that it was done "by dropping five cents in the slot." Anyone who has actually travelled our humid old Hudson Tube knows well that it costs a dime; and it isn't a slot, but a sort of perforated catch-all in which your money makes a delicious tinkling. This same jovial pretender did himself gruesome wrong by describing the Hoboken resorts, which he plainly had never seen, as "quaint," with "candles on the tables." He was mixing us up with Greenwich Village. There isn't room on a Hoboken tavern table for any candles; and "quaint," thank God, is the last thing Hoboken will ever be. It's rowdy; and we could tell you stories to prove it . . . stories that will never get into print.

But anyhow, here are a few of the remarks that have amused us, so much so that we wanted to preserve them for affectionate contemplation. Let's begin with the first and earliest of the lot, from the New York *Times* of August 14, 1928:—

THEATRE BY FERRY

"If the plans of the Hoboken Theatrical Company materialize, that city will be avenged upon New York for the vaudeville jokes of sev-

Seidel over to Hoboken
And see
MORLEY
GRIBBLE
THROCKMORTON
HOBOKEN 8088
NEW YORK'S
LAST
SEACOAST
OF BOHEMIA
RIALTO THEATRE
118 Hudson street
HOBOKEN
Seven nights a week
at 8:30
MILLIKEN

eral generations. For these plans, as gingerly discussed by CHRISTOPHER MORLEY, include the leasing of the old Rialto Theatre at Hoboken and stock company production of new plays and recent Broadway successes.

"With Mr. MORLEY are to be associated CLEON THROCKMORTON and CONRAD MILLIKEN, and the presence of all three suggests that the Twenty-third Street ferries may carry loads of esthetes to Hoboken, fleeing the materialism of New York. That would be Hoboken's revenge for such jokes as: 'Have you ever been in Hoboken?' 'No, aren't we at war with those people?'

"Mr. MORLEY was not quite ready to tell all when a reporter from THE TIMES approached him; and he added that there would be a very 'interesting story' to be related when plans are more matured. Many New Yorkers who often make the Hoboken pilgrimage because of the especial coldness and vivacity of the near-beer dispensed in that city will hope that the 'interesting story' may deal with a merger of Gambrinus and Thalia. Even if it is only near-beer, how pleasant (they muse) it would be to sit around palm-bedecked tables during entr'-actes again."

St. John Ervine in *The World* (Oct. 22, 1928):—

". . . . immediately I knew that I was in a place frequented by sailors. I recognized that port-y smell, that port-y appearance, which exhilarate me whenever I find myself anywhere near a harbor. All the odors of all the ships that ever steamed or sailed were mingling in that delicious air, and when I looked at men walking on the pavements—I beg your pardon! sidewalks —I saw a slight roll in their gait that was due not to the blessings of Prohibition but to the heaving of boats and the tilt of the sea.

". . . . in the Hoboken Hofbrau, I ate a meal that made Morley feel ashamed of me. He approved of me supping clam chowder, and when I had tasted a spoonful of it I approved of myself for supping it. But he considered me to be a low fellow when I called for and persisted in eating a dish which, despite the delicacy of my readers, I must name: pig's knuckle and red cabbage. I know that since my arrival in New York a legend has gone all over the United States that The World is now a very tony paper, with culture fairly dripping from my column, but I cannot continue to be a whited sepulchre any longer. The truth must be told, and it is this: I am passionately fond of vulgar food. Morley cannot eat tripe, which shows what sort of an author he is..I love it. Onions are not my only joy, but they rank high. (I draw attention to the witticism in the last sentence.) And I devoured that pig's knuckle and red cabbage with a relish that only great and accomplished eaters experience.

"There was a man called Milliken at the table who gave himself airs by professing to be as fond of vulgar food as I am, and, as I believe, out of sheer bravado he too ordered a dish of pig's knuckle and red cabbage. But what a poor performance was his! He toyed with the meat and tried to. persuade Morley to taste some of it in the pretense that he would share his pleasure with him, when all he wanted to do was to reduce the quantity he had to eat. I left him still protesting that he loved the dish, but there was a look in his eye which belied him.

"And now I found myself in the most adventurous part of my journey. I was led up to an old theatre, called the Rialto. The drop curtain reminded me of the first drop curtain I ever saw, although the picture in the middle of it was not a fine view of the Lakes of Killarney but a fine view of two ladies who had taken off all their clothes so that they might talk to each other. At the Rialto, I found a group of young actors and actresses gallantly building up a theatre which will appeal to the whole of Hoboken and not to a small, self-conscious section of it. The play, perhaps, was simpler than it need have been, simpler, certainly, than the players' abilities required it to be, but it was good-natured stuff and it pleased the audience. The company was excellent and it had the air, which young players ought to possess, of enjoying its job.

"There is a theatre in Liverpool, the Playhouse, which began as the Rialto in Hoboken

ILLYRISCHES NATIONAL LIED

Words by Christopher Morley

Jerome Kern

has begun. It is now the most prosperous theatre of its kind in Great Britain. Plays here are performed for at least a fortnight, and are sometimes performed for as long as four or five weeks. I doubt if it is possible to obtain in Liverpool such a gaudy meal as I got in Hoboken. I wish that it were. Those of my readers who are informing me in their thousands that they are heartily sick of the cocktail, cuss-and-kill drama now flourishing on Broadway can comfort themselves with better stuff at the Rialto. They may some day (and soon, perhaps) be able to boast that they were in at the beginnings of the Hoboken theatre, as some people, myself among them, claim credit for themselves because they were in at the beginnings of the Theatre Guild of New York."

Mr. J. Brooks Atkinson, in the NEW YORK TIMES:—

"According to the legend—for everything about their fantastic enterprise is legendary—Mr. Throckmorton first discovered this quiet old playhouse 'on the last seacoast of Bohemia' and coveted it for art as well as sentiment. Mr.

Seidel Over to Hoboken

New York's Last Seacoast of Bohemia

The Old Rialto Theatre, 118 Hudson Street, Hoboken

Opening TONIGHT, November 26th, and for TWO WEEKS, that Synopsis of Sentiment and Schmerz, Classic of Wine, Woman and Song.

OLD HEIDELBERG

produced in surroundings worthy of its charm

Only 3 blocks from Lackawanna Terminal. Ferries (Barclay St., Christopher St., 23rd St.) to Lackawanna; or Hudson Tubes to Hoboken. EVERY evening, including Sunday, at 8.30. Matinees Tuesday and Saturday, 2:30. Top prices 99c and $1.25.

Phone HOBOKEN 8088 for reservations and advice.

Save this valuable memorandum. You know perfectly well we can't afford to advertise often. Gaudeamus igitur..........

Morley, Throckmorton, Milliken, Gribble

The Old Rialto Theatre, Hoboken

(She Troupes to Conquer)

and a dozen ancillary and adjacent inns, still have room, Tonight and Every Night, for about 317 New Yorkers who might relish pernoctations of mirth unknown elsewhere. If you intend to be one of those 317, call HOBOKEN 8088 for reservations and advice. Box office open 11 A. M.

Tonight and Tomorrow, BROADWAY (last 3 times)

November 26th, and for TWO WEEKS, that barytone classic of Sentiment and Schmerz, that idol with feet of Bertha Clay, OLD HEIDELBERG, of which C. E. Montague said: "3 Hours' Revel. We lie and wallow in it as wallowing narwhals love the deep."

Speaking, as someone was, of Places to Go Sunday Evening, THE OLD RIALTO, HOBOKEN, is Perfectly Amusing. . . .

Save this precious intimation. You know perfectly well we can't afford to advertise often.

The Old Rialto Theatre, 118 Hudson Street, Hoboken 20 minutes: ferry to Lackawanna, or Hudson Tubes to Hoboken.

Morley, Throckmorton, Milliken, Gribble

The Old Rialto Theatre, Hoboken

New York's Last Seacoast of Bohemia

ALL THIS WEEK, including next Sunday, 2d and Final Week of

OLD HEIDELBERG

Sheridan, 150 years away, wrote the Perfect Theatre Advertisement. It applies accurately to our production of Old Heidelberg:

We are at a loss which to admire most, the unrivalled genius of the author, the great attention and liberality of the managers, the wonderful abilities of the scene-painter, or the incredible exertions of all the performers.

(The Critic, 1779)

Reservations NOW for our Sensational Holiday Anomaly, opening DECEMBER 10: the Revival Riotous of

AFTER DARK: or NEITHER MAID, WIFE, NOR WIDOW

Famous Melodrama of 1868, played in its own manner.

☞ Prices RAISED to $2 and $1 for this Special Opening Night.

The house seats only 700. Be Advised. Telephone HOBOKEN 8088.

The Old Rialto Theatre, 118 Hudson Street, Hoboken

Only 20 minutes. Ferries to Lackawanna or Hudson Tubes to Hoboken. Save this costly inuendo. You know perfectly well we cannot afford to advertise often.

Morley, Throckmorton, Milliken, Gribble

OPENING TONIGHT

At the Old Rialto Theatre, 118 Hudson Street, Hoboken
that prime elixir of the Bowery and demiurge of drama

AFTER DARK

OR, NEITHER MAID, WIFE, NOR WIDOW

Famous melodrama of 1868, faithfully exhumed and played in its own manner, in a pagan playhouse of its own era.

This, our Sensational Holiday Anomaly, provides the Most Amusing Escapade in New York. Bookings NOW for Holiday parties. TONIGHT, for this Lustrous Opening, prices RAISED to $2 and $1. Thereafter, every evening (including Sunday) and matinees Tuesday and Saturday, our grotesquely modest tariff of $1.25, 99c, 75c. Curtain 8.30 sharp. Phone Hoboken 8088 for information.

New York's Last Seacoast of Bohemia

20 Minutes: Ferries to Lackawanna or Hudson Tubes.

☞ Cherish this precious memo. You know perfectly well we can't afford to advertise often.

Morley, Throckmorton, Milliken, Gribble

Born in a Beer Garden

in 1863, the Old Rialto Theatre, 118 Hudson St., Hoboken, deserves to be a permanent institution among the better merriments of New York.

If you see that pagan old playhouse as we do, New York's Last Seacoast of Bohemia, still unspoiled by Psittacine and Psophist, pass on the jocund word. Make the odyssey of the oddities; seidel over to Hoboken and see. It won't be long now... Gentlemen, our mistress, the Old Rialto Theatre. Prosit! She's toasted!

Only 20 minutes from 33rd St. by Hudson Tubes. You can read Wiener Schnitzler on the way, and eat them when you get there. HOBOKEN 8088 for reservations. And don't leave it too late.

Week of Oct. 22, THE OCTOPUS
Week of Oct. 29, PLEASED TO MEET YOU

(Premiere, with sensational music by Jerome Kern)

Save this memo. You know perfectly well we can't afford to advertise often.

Morley, Throckmorton, Milliken, Gribble

Forgive Us

for not being able to satisfy all demands for seats at the opening to-night of

PLEASED TO MEET YOU

A new comedy by Christopher Morley

but our proletarian old Rialto cannot comfortably hold more than about 900 sedentary customers.

To prevent disappointment we have arranged to run this play for TWO WEEKS. Performances of increasing dexterity EVERY evening and matinees Tuesday and Saturday.

Many do not believe it can really be true: A LAST SEACOAST OF BOHEMIA, unspoiled by Psittacine and Psophist, only 20 minutes away by Hudson Tube or ferry. 99 cents top.

Our announcements are necessarily sparse, meagre, unconvincing. You know perfectly well we can't afford to advertise often. Seidel over and see. HOBoken 8088.

Please do not embarrass us by wearing evening dress.

Old Rialto Theatre, 118 Hudson Street, Hoboken

Morley swears along toward midnight that every brick 'sings with memories.'

"Certainly no theatre was ever operated on more genial terms. As Mr. Throckmorton explains, the Hoboken location saves these light-minded playboys from being real estate gamblers, as most New York theatre lessees have to be, or myrmidons of the ambitious arts, like the hide-away theatres of Manhattan. As managers of a stock theatre they can divide their time between new plays and the old Broadway buncombe, with only their audience and themselves to consult. Even if the Old Rialto does not succeed, it is apparent that its managers are not overwhelmed by the gravity of their task. The Hofbräu is near by, dwarfed by steamship spars at the foot of the street. The Continental Hotel is across the way. Round the corner is the Travelers' Rest. Indeed, one is now and then astonished to find grocery stores, hardware shops and other matter-of-fact institutions still open for business in this foaming, amber community. The program declares, 'You are always sure of good entertainment at the Old Rialto, bless its ancient boards.' Or across the street, bless its stained tables.

"Although the Old Rialto has been painted and freshened, it still wears the honorable scars of use. Initials carved in the woodwork by rascals still show through the new paint; and the steps have been hollowed by many impatient feet. The brick walls date from some sixty or seventy years ago, when the Rialto was put up as part of the Elysian Fields where 'on a warm Summer afternoon or on a moonlit evening, might be seen scores of both sexes strolling upon the soft grass, or sitting upon the greensward, recalling to memory many beautiful sketches of life in the earlier periods of the world, given in the volumes of old poets.' Perhaps those were the blissful, bucolic days when Mary Rogers, the beautiful tobacco-girl, was mysteriously murdered in the Elysian Fields, giving Poe a ready-made plot for the 'Mystery of Marie Roget.' At any rate, not all the Elysian Fielders were fastidious promenaders. Early in the present century Manhattaners found convenient places there for relieving the legal aridities of Sunday.

"At about the same time the old 'Rye-alto,' as the local folk pronounce it, was remodeled in its present form with a dignified proscenium arch, finely carved balcony and gallery balustrades and rococo scrolls as the traditional decoration."

"Lipstick," in *The New Yorker:—*

"Somehow Hoboken doesn't seem far away to me now, with the Holland Tunnel and all. This was where I took myself for a slight vacation. For, when the intelligentsia discover a place, you may be certain that the cooking is not only good, but amusing; that, in that subtle thing known as atmosphere, you are suddenly made to feel like laughing, and talking, and tearing the world apart to find out what's wrong with the carburetor. In Hoboken they are not refined. They understand steaks and schnitzel, and the correct measurements for a helping of caviar."

R. Dana Skinner, in *The Commonweal:—*

"They have so much fun doing the impossible that the spirit of it floods across the footlights and leaves you utterly charmed and highly uncritical."

David McCord, in the Boston *Transcript:*—

"I remember a very soft October evening, full of Manhattan brume and the mobile lights of the North River. A ferry took us over from Twenty-third Street to the Lackawanna terminals. (This is the recommended route to the Rialto, though you can switch your New York dock to Christopher Street if you prefer it). The four tall spars of an old schooner lifted out of the night beside us as we walked the block or so to Hudson Street. I thought of Emerson: 'This very street of hucksters and taverns the moon will transform to a Palmyra.' It was all strangely quiet—a kind of Hoboken hush—when over the way, under what web of lights and foggy plumes, sounded the rumble of a great city. Three minutes took us to the beginning of a continental meal. An hour and we were in the theatre.

"People who own etchings of Canal Street when it was a canal, who still care to walk over

Brooklyn Bridge, or ferry to Staten Island, or cruise about the greensward of Battery Park, will appreciate what these venturers have done."

Julius Hands Us The Key, August, 1928

During the early weeks of the season the company of players included the following artists:—

ALLYN GILLYN, ISABEL BARING, MARCIA HANAN, VIOLET GALE, JESSIE GRAHAM, GERTRUDE RITCHIE, DOROTHY LEWIS, BLIX RUSKAY, CATHERINE DAVIES, PHYLLIS BERGLIN, MARY THAYER, PRISCILLA SHINDEL, EUNICE HOWARD, WINONA WALTHALL, CYRENA SMITH, E. EVANS, BEATRICE HOLTBY.

DENNIS CLEUGH*, ARTHUR C. MORRIS, JOHN REGAN, JOHN NEGLEY, ALEXANDER CLARK JR., CECIL HOLM, BRADLEY CASS, GILBERT SQUAREY, ALAN FLOUD, THOMAS KILMARTIN, JOSEPH THAYER, VERNON RICH, ARTHUR KNEERIM, RALPH ROBINSON, PAT O'BRIEN, GORDON HURD, A. ANGELL, L. MARKOVYN, JO LEON, F. HART, C. ASHTON, IVAN PAULL, CHRIS HOWLEY.

---

*Deceased, November 2, 1928.

THE OLD

RIALTO THEATRE

Under Management of

CHRISTOPHER MORLEY **HARRY WAGSTAFF GRIBBLE**
CLEON THROCKMORTON **CONRAD MILLIKEN**

CHRISTOPHER MORLEY	*President*
CLEON THROCKMORTON	*Vice President*
CONRAD MILLIKEN	*Treasurer*
HARRY WAGSTAFF GRIBBLE	*Director*
E. S. COLLING	*Company Manager*
MIRIAM LIPTON	*Assistant*
CHARLES MILLER	*Musical Adviser*
ARTHUR WYMAN	*Technical Director*
LAWRENCE BOLTON	*Associate Stage Director and Stage Manager*
GEORGE MEEKER	*House Manager*
THOMAS KILMARTIN	*Asst. House Manager*
ALFRED BURKE	*Asst. Stage Manager*
ELEANOR AUGUSTE	*Cashier*
TOM ADRIAN CRACRAFT	*Scenic Artist*
GENE BEALL	*Stage Carpenter*
RICHARD HANCOX	*Asst. Stage Carpenter*
WILLIAM QUINN	*Property Master*
MARTIN JOHNSON	*Asst. Property Master*
HENRY KUNTZE	*Electrician*
JAMES HILLIS	*Flyman*
SAM TAUSEND	*Orchestra Director*
FRED GANSLEY	*Special Officer*

jay